I0470986

DELIVERY SERVICES

Second Edition

7 Steps to a Medical Cannabis Business

Editor: Douglas Slain, M.A., J.D.

Table of Contents

Publisher: The Law Offices of Douglas Slain

59 Morning Sun Avenue, Suite A
Mill Valley, CA 94104
T: 415-888-8289 / F: 415-383-1766
E: lawyer@thedefenselawyer.com

About the Author

Douglas Slain represents criminal defendants in marijuana cases throughout Northern California and he also prepares exempt offerings for real estate blind pools in California and elsewhere. His law firm also represents investors in California private offerings.

Slain has previously published *Insurance Litigation Reporter, Professional Liability Reporter, Securities Enforcement Reporter, Construction Litigation Reporter, Blue Sky Chronicle, Medical Liability Reporter, Verdicts &Settlements*, and *Bad Faith Digest*. Some of these titles are now published by Thomson-Reuters. Slain now writes and teaches in the fields of a) exempt offerings and securities law and b) cannabis commerce law and practice.

Slain has served as a chair for a large ABA professional responsibility committee for two years; he also served in Riga as a secured transaction adviser to the Ministry of Economy. He taught real estate transactions to Stanford Law students as an adjunct clinical law professor for one semester. Slain received a MA in History from the University of Chicago and a JD from Stanford Law School. He has two children and he lives in Mill Valley. He has two signs on his desk.

"The Life of the Land is Perpetuated in Righteousness"-Hawaii state motto since 1956, author unknown.

"Be kind, for everyone you meet is fighting a great battle." Philo, 3rd century BC Jewish philosopher

Chapter One: Seven Steps to a Medical Cannabis Business

AFTER YOU HAVE STUDIED LOCAL POLITICS, ORDINANCES, ZONING AND TALKED TO PEOPLE WHO KNOW WHAT IS GOING ON.

1. OBTAIN STATE ID CARD

2. NAME; PHONE AND FAX LINES; BUSINESS ADDRESS; URL

3. FORM YOUR NON-PROFIT

4. ESTABLISH BANK ACCOUNT AND OBTAIN A FEIN NUMBER

5. GET SELLER'S PERMIT

6. GET BUSINESS LICENSE

7. PURCHASE PATIENT SOFTWARE

FIRST: HOW ABOUT THE MONEY?

Posit:

8 deliveries per day on average working 6 days each week (taking off Monday for instance) with average purchase ½ oz. for $100 =$19,200

Cost of product: $13,300 or 7 pounds @ $1,900/pound.

$19,200 average monthly income

$13,300 cost of goods

$5,900 for estimated quarterly taxes; all overhead and all costs, including yourself

12 x $5,900 = $70,800 annual gross *taxable* income

STEP ONE

STATE ID CARD

Contact The Department of Health and Human Resources in your county. (http://www.cdph.ca.gov/programs/MMP/) issues the state ID card which identifies you as a patient and/or caregiver.

A caregiver card allows you to carry a given amount of marijuana for each person in your care. Start by downloading the form at www.cdph.ca.gov/programs/mmp

To apply as a Medical Marijuana Program (MMP) patient in person, you will need your personal information as well as your physician's contact information, license number, and licensing board.

Be prepared to:

Prove residency (in county of application) with a driver's license, rent or mortgage slip, or utility bill.

Prove your identity with a government-issued photo ID or a certified copy of your birth certificate

Pay application fees.

Be photographed by your county agency.

As a caregiver, you need a patient to designate you as their primary caregiver. Supposedly, you also must show that you care for "the core survival needs" of your patient before his/her need for marijuana arose.

Remember: If you register as the primary caregiver for more than one patient, you must live in the same county as all patients.

You can locate your county's office at Http://www.Cdph.ca.gov/services/Pages/MMP Counties.aspx

For the office visit, the patient must be present, whether applying with a caregiver or not. If the patient already has a card, he/she will need to present it for the care giver's application. If the patient receives Medical, the fee for both the caregiver and patient is reduced 50%.

STEP TWO

NAME, CONTACT INFORMATION, URL

Create a business name; perhaps with 'patient' or 'caregiver' or 'collective' in it.

Your physical address must be in the city and county you will be serving. It cannot be a PO box.

Create a web site or URL. Part of establishing your delivery service is creating a brand for yourself. If you don't have a storefront to represent yourself, a website allows people to see what benefits you offer them.

First secure a domain name. Once you have something descriptive (words such as "patient", "caregiver", or "collective" are good) go to a domain registry (such as godaddy.com or register.com) and see if it is available. If so, you can pay a small fee to claim your name.

Then find a service to host the web site you create under your domain name. There are plenty of companies that offer hosting space and design tools so that you can put your domain to good use, and they usually do not cost much. (I use vistaprint.com's services).

STEP THREE

FORM NON-PROFIT

The least expensive and easiest way to get going is to create a member-operator collective in the form of an unincorporated non-profit association.

You can set things up so that, although you are the president, you are also a "member operator" and therefore not responsible for the actions of other members.

Your membership agreement will set forth the rules for the membership; you and/or your lawyer will write those rules; no one can join unless she or he has signed an original of this membership agreement.

You need to create by-laws and other corporate documentation. To start, google secState Form LP/UNA 128, and send in $10 with the name of your non-profit.

STEP FOUR

ESTABLISH BANK ACCOUNT; GET A FEIN NUMBER

Go to your bank and set up a business account.

You will need all your documentation, including non-profit documentation.

To qualify for a seller's permit, you will need a FEIN or EIN number. You can obtain your EIN from the IRS by phone, mail, fax, or online.

You will need to provide information on your business, including the legal name and structure and mailing address. You can download the form ahead of time at http://www.irs.gov/pub/irs-pdf/fss4.pdf.

To receive your EIN online, visit http://www.IRS.gov/businesses/small/article/0,,id=102767,00.htm

The site will ask you questions, and then issue your EIN immediately, but it only takes requests

Monday through Friday, 8am to 5pm Eastern Standard Time.

If you call the Business & Specialty Tax Line at (800) 829-4933 and answer the operator's questions, you can receive your EIN immediately.

To receive your EIN by fax, print and fill out the SS-4 form then fax it to (859) 669-5760. Provide a return phone number and your EIN will be faxed back within 4 business days. You can print out the SS-4 form and mail it to:

Internal Revenue Service
Attn: EIN Operation
Cincinnati, OH 45999

This method will take 4 weeks to process. To find out more, see http//: www.IRS.gov/businesses/small/articleOvid=978 60, 00.html; or go to irs.gov, and then click "Businesses", then "Small Business/Self Employed."

You will need your non-profit papers and be prepared to pay a minimum deposit to establish your account.

STEP FIVE

SELLER'S PERMIT

Seller's permits are obtained from the California State Board of Equalization.

With your bank account information and other documentation in hand, go to the local office of the Board of Equalization and use the new business checking account to sign a check for a down payment.

You will need to estimate your quarterly income.

STEP SIX

BUSINESS LICENSE

Google "business license" under the name of your town. Download the form if possible. Go to their office and bring all of your documents. Tell them you will be operating a home health-care delivery service from your chosen address.

STEP SEVEN

PATIENT SOFTWARE

Go online and search for patient software. There are several good options. You can purchase software or just a license, using offshore servers.

Among other reasons you want this software is to keep track of your patients' buying habits and contact information.

Chapter Two: Operations

Membership Application &Verification

To join your group each new member must complete a written membership application.

Application Requirements

Verify the individual's status as a qualified patient or care giver. Unless he or she has a state medical marijuana identification card, you need to make personal contact with the recommending physician's office. Copies should be made of any physician's recommendation or identification card.

Written commitment not to use marijuana for other than medical purposes must be signed. You should maintain membership records on-site or have them reasonably available so as track when members' medical marijuana recommendation and/or identification cards expire.

Acquire Lawfully Cultivated Marijuana

Collectives and cooperatives should acquire marijuana only from their constituent members. Only marijuana grown by a qualified patient or his or her primary caregiver may lawfully be distributed to other members of a collective or cooperative. The collective or cooperative then distributes it to other members of the group. The cycle should be a closed.

Reimbursements and Allocations

Members may reimburse the collective or cooperative for marijuana that has been allocated to them. Any monetary reimbursement that members provide to them collective or cooperative should only be an amount necessary to cover overhead costs and operating expenses.

Marijuana grown at a collective or cooperative for medical purposes may be provided free to qualified patients and primary care givers who are members of the collective or cooperative; provided in exchange for services rendered to the entity; allocated based on fees that are reasonably calculated to cover overhead costs and operating expenses; or d) any combination of the above.

Possession and Cultivation

A patient/collective member/primary caregiver may aggregate the possession and cultivation limits for each patient. If you are in possession of more than your personal amount of medical marijuana, you should have supporting records readily available, especially when transporting medical marijuana.

Security

Collectives and cooperatives should provide adequate security to ensure that patients are safe and that the surrounding homes or businesses are not negatively impacted by nuisance activity such as loitering.

Chapter Three: Primary Caregivers

The California Supreme Court has set forth the requirements for a primary caregiver: primary caregiver: An individual who consistently provides care giving, independent of any assistance in taking medical marijuana, at or before the time he or she assumed responsibility for assisting with medical marijuana." *People v. Mentch (2008) 45 Cal.4th 274, 283 (85 Cal. Rptr. 3d 480, 195 P.3d 1061).* The person must show "a caretaking relationship directed at the core survival needs of a seriously ill patient, not just one single pharmaceutical need." *Id.* at p. 286.

Growers may serve as caregivers under certain circumstances. **Caregivers can serve more than one patient, but patients can have only one primary caregiver.**

NORML recommends that caregiver growers limit the number of patients they serve:

In general the courts have held that cannabis clubs cannot serve as primary caregivers for large numbers of patients, but a caregiver may serve more than one patient. Some persons claim caregiver status while growing for multiple numbers of patients on the theory that they are providing for their health and safety. This argument has been successful in court for caregivers growing for small numbers of patients.

Caregiver-growers should limit themselves to a select membership list of patients whom they personally know and who do not have other caregivers.

SB 420 allows caregivers to be compensated for the costs of their services, but it does not authorize the sale of marijuana itself for profit.

How much marijuana can be grown and distributed by caregivers?

Caregivers and patients can band together in a coop or collective and grow and distribute to the members the total amount allowed divided by the number of members.

In *People v Urziceanu* (*2005 Third Appellate District*) *132 Cal.App.4th 747*, the Court ruled that, while Prop. 215 did not authorize distribution by anyone except primary caregivers, SB 420 allowed for distribution among patients and caregivers through collectives and cooperatives.

NORML argues that:

"*The question remains as to how much medical marijuana cooperatives and collectives are allowed to grow or possess. According to the AG's guidelines, they can scale the SB 420 limits in proportion to the number of their members.*

"*For example, under the standard state guideline, a coop with ten members could have ten times the limits, i.e. 60 mature or120 immature plants and up to 80 ounces of marijuana. However, some counties and cities have established a maximum cap on the size of collective gardens: for example, San Francisco does not allow more than 99 plants in any case.*"

The law is confusing, especially because of a recent California Supreme Court decision outlawing limitations on the amount of marijuana that can be grown or distributed. Thus, **permissible distribution has been expanded and confused by the decision**. *People v. Kelly,*

(2010) 47 Cal. 4th 1008), holds that the parts of SB 420 setting limits on the amount of marijuana a patient or caregiver may grow are an unconstitutional amendment to the voters' initiative.

NORML draws a distinction between preventing arrest and prevailing in court. It advises growers to prevent arrest by adhering to the limits of the provisions of 420 – 6 mature plants and 8 oz of dried marijuana bud or equivalent, even though at trial, they may prevail.

Bottom line: **SB 420 guidelines are not legally determinative of guilt in court, but that they can still be used by law enforcement as guidelines for when to arrest people.** In the meantime, growers are advised to adhere to the guidelines to the extent possible and as practicable.

IN SUMMARY:

Patients can have any amount of cannabis consistent with their personal medical needs.

Patients and caregivers with a state-issued ID card are immune from arrest and allowed to possess whatever amount the law allows them.

Patients and caregivers without a state-issued card, even with a physician's statement or county entitlement, are subject to case by case scrutiny. P

Patients may keep gardens of whatever size and take dosages of any amount, or at least their lawyers can argue that in court but staying within the guidelines significantly reduces likelihood of criminal charges.

The default setting is always the state's guidelines under Health & Safety Code set a minimum of 6 mature plants or 12 immature ones and up to 8 ounces of processed cannabis bud or flower, although a physician's letter permits larger amounts and both cities and counties are empowered to set guidelines that are greater than these amounts (but not less!).

NB: If it ever happens that you are charged with intent to sell, make sure your lawyer pays careful attention to Health and Safety Code subsection 11362.

Chapter Four: State California Cannabis Law

Many California Health and Safety Code sections regarding possession and cultivation of marijuana do not apply to patients or patients' care givers *who possess or cultivate marijuana for the personal medical use of a patient on the recommendation of a physician.*

California has in fact decriminalized marijuana to the extent that first-time felony offenders are no longer going to state prison unless there is something else going on.

It is not as though you are not operating on the edge of the law, however. Aside from a claimed medical marijuana defense, it remains the case that although possession of up to 28.5 grams is no longer enough for the police to arrest you, they can make you appear in court, charge you with a misdemeanor, and get you find you $100.

Meanwhile, if a deputy DA decides at any time to charge you with another *merely alleged* crime — even unrelated, or if he just wants to cause you trouble, the California's Health and Safety and Criminal codes continue to say that:

a) cultivation
b) processing, and
c) sales of marijuana

are all punishable as felonies!

Possession of more than 28.5 grams remains punishable by up to 6 months in jail, and giving away less than 28.5 grams is a misdemeanor. And of course, any sale of marijuana to a minor is a felony. Possession of 28.5 grams or less on school grounds when the school is open is punishable by up to 10 days in jail and a $500 fine.

More grams than that? Felony.

Anyone under the age of 21 who is convicted of any 420-related offense will have his or her driver's license suspended for up to one year. Possession of paraphernalia is a civil offense, with a fine of $300 for first offense and more thereafter.

Chapter Five: County Guidelines

NB: The author encourages readers to communicate any and all corrections and updates directly with him (editor@lawandpractice.com) as these guidelines are truly a moving target.

Alameda: 6 mature plants or 12 immature plants & 8 ounces of bud

Alpine: 6 mature plants or 12 immature plants & 8 ounces of bud

Amador: 6 mature plants or 12 immature plants & 8 ounces of bud

Butte: 6 mature plants or 12 immature plants & one pound of processed (formerly 6 plants at any stage)

Calaveras: 6 mature plants or 12 immature plants & 8 ounces of bud

Colusa: No firm policy; case-by-case review, though "tentative guidelines" of 6 mature plants or 12 immature plants & 8 ounces of bud or 1.5

lb. processed (formerly 2 plants outdoors or 4 plants indoors)

Contra Costa: 6 mature plants or 12 immature plants & 8 ounces of bud

Del Norte: Current status remains cloudy, so follow the state minimum guidelines for maximum safety: 6 mature plants or 12 immature plants & 8 ounces of bud.

El Dorado: **Outdoors:** 20 plants from March 1 through July 31; 10 plants through October (or end of season); 2 lbs. of bud from September 1 through February 28; and 1 lb from March 1 to August 31. **Indoors:** 10 vegetative plants, 1 mother plant, 10 flowering plants and 1 lb of bud per patient (formerly 6 plants and/or 2 pounds processed). NB: Caregivers can take care of household plus three outside patients. Also see El Dorado County DA Policy.

Fresno: 6 mature plants or 12 immature plants & 8 ounces of bud

Glenn: 6 mature plants or 12 immature plants & 8 ounces of bud

Humboldt: 3 lbs of bud or equivalent; 100 square feet of garden canopy, no limit on plant numbers or lamp wattage. Caregiver amounts calculated per patient served. [Original DA policy: Up to 99 plants with up to 100 square feet of canopy and up to lb. of bud. **Indoor** gardens limited to 1500 watts total illumination.]

Imperial: 6 mature plants or 12 immature plants & 8 ounces of bud

Inyo: 6 mature plants or 12 immature plants & 8 ounces of bud

Kern: 6 mature plants or 12 immature plants & 8 ounces of bud.

King: 6 mature plants or 12 immature plants & 8 ounces of bud
Lake: 6 mature plants or 12 immature plants & 8 ounces of bud

Lassen: 6 mature plants or 12 immature plants & 8 ounces of bud

Los Angeles: 6 mature plants or 12 immature plants & 8 ounces of bud

Madera: 6 mature plants or 12 immature plants & 8 ounces of bud

Marin: 6 mature plants or 12 immature plants & 8 ounces of bud, county ID cards now honored by all law enforcement.

Mariposa: 6 mature plants or 12 immature plants & 8 ounces of bud

Mendocino: Measure 'B' to revert to the statewide minimum guidelines of 6 mature plants or 12 immature plants & 8 ounces was suspended but has again been implemented (for now)

Merced: 6 mature plants or 12 immature plants & 8 ounces of bud

Modoc: 6 mature plants or 12 immature plants & 8 ounces of bud

Mono: 6 mature plants or 12 immature plants & 8 ounces of bud

Monterey: 6 mature plants or 12 immature plants & 8 ounces of bud

Napa: 6 mature plants or 12 immature plants & 8 ounces of bud

Nevada: 6 mature plants or 12 immature plants any size; or, in the alternative, 75 square feet of total canopy area & up to 2 lb. of bud. Collectives must keep copies of all patients' recommendations available for inspection.

Orange: 6 mature plants or 12 immature plants & 8 ounces of bud

Placer: 6 mature plants or 12 immature plants & 8 ounces of bud

Plumas: 6 mature plants or 12 immature plants & 8 ounces of bud

Riverside: 6 mature plants or 12 immature plants & 8 ounces of bud

Sacramento: 6 mature plants or 12 immature plants & 8 ounces of bud

San Benito: 6 mature plants or 12 immature plants & 8 ounces of bud

San Bernardino: 6 mature plants or 12 immature plants & 8 ounces of bud

San Diego: 6 mature plants or 12 immature plants & 8 ounces of bud

San Francisco: Patient and caregiver ID cards issued by county Health Department; no patient guidelines. Case by case policy is based on police claims of indicia of illegal sales or diversion to non-medical market.

San Joaquin: 6 mature plants or 12 immature plants & 8 ounces of bud

San Luis Obispo: 6 mature plants or 12 immature plants & 8 ounces of bud

San Mateo: 6 mature plants or 12 immature plants & 8 ounces of bud

Santa Barbara: 6 mature plants or 12 immature plants & 8 ounces of bud

Santa Clara: 6 mature plants or 12 immature plants & 8 ounces of bud

Santa Cruz: 3 pounds of bud or equivalent, plus 100 square feet of garden canopy, no limit on plant numbers or lamp wattage

Shasta: 6 mature plants or 12 immature plants & 8 ounces of bud or 1.33 lb. processed

Sierra: 6 mature plants or 12 immature plants & 8 ounces of bud or any quantity approved by physician

Siskiyou: 6 mature plants or 12 immature plants & 8 ounces of bud

Solano: 6 mature plants or 12 immature plants & 8 ounces of bud

Sonoma: County policy: Up to 30 plants with up to 100 square feet of garden canopy and up to 3 lb. of bud.

Stanislaus: 6 mature plants or 12 immature plants and 8 ounces of bud

Sutter: 6 mature plants or 12 immature plants & 8 ounces of bud

Tehama: 12 seedlings or 6 flowering or mature plants, and 8 ounces dried marijuana. Indoor Cultivation: 12 seedlings or 6 flowering or mature plants, and 8 ounces dried marijuana.

Trinity: Board of Supervisors voted to step backward and revert to the state minimum threshold of 6 mature plants or 12 immature plant & 8 ounces of bud

Tulare: 6 mature plants or 12 immature plants & 8 ounces of bud

Tuolumne: 6 mature plants or 12 immature plants & 8 ounces of bud.

Ventura: 6 mature plants or 12 immature plants & 8 ounces of bud or 1 lb. dry bud or conversion.

Yolo: 6 mature plants or 12 immature plants & 8 ounces of bud

Yuba: Informal policy: 6 mature plants or 12 immature plants & 8 ounces of bud or 1.5 lb. of processed marijuana.

Chapter Six: Federal Cannabis Law

California does not enforce Federal Criminal Statutes; (see *People v. Telehkooh*) *"It is not the job of the local police to enforce the Federal drug law as such."* (*Garden v. Superior Court*)

However, Federal law cannot be ignored; consequences in the Federal forum are severe and the Department of Justice and the IRS (as well as other Federal agencies) continue to harass the industry.

The DEA prohibits cultivation of cannabis and manufacture and dispensing of by placing them in a Schedule I category.

Doctors are forbidden to *prescribe* cannabis, but they can *recommend* or *approve* its use.
They cannot help patients obtain it. However, *Marinol*™, a synthetic THC in gel capsule form, is available by prescription as a Schedule III drug.

Penalties for possessing a federal controlled substance may include up to a year in prison, a fine, or both. Subsequent violations: 90 days to three years plus a fine.

Action or conspiracy to cultivate up to 50 plants or distribute up to 50 kilograms of cannabis, 10 kilos of hash, or one kilo of hash oil draw fines and a sentence up to five years.

More than 100 kilos or 100 plants: a mandatory five-year sentence. For 1000 kilos or 1000 plants, a mandatory 10 years, plus fines.

Property including real estate, money, vehicles, securities or other things of value that can be connected to violations of federal drug law are subject to confiscation by the US government (21 USC 841, 844, 844a, 881).

There is currently no medical marijuana exception. However, the Ninth Circuit affirmed a physician's First Amendment right to treat a patient without fear of arrest in *Conant v. Walters;* (9th Cir 2002) 309 F.3d 629.
The ruling enjoins the federal government from revoking a physician's license for prescribing controlled substances or conducting an investigation of a physician that might lead to such revocation—where the basis for the government's action is solely the physician's professional 'recommendation' of the use of

medical marijuana.

The ruling has been said to show how the government's professed enforcement policy threatens to interfere with expressions protected by the First Amendment.

US v. Oakland Cannabis Buyers' Coop. stands for that the doctrine of "medical necessity" does not give marijuana providers a defense against federal distribution charges, even within state borders to seriously ill patients.

The court wrote,

[T]he Controlled Substances Act reflects a determination that marijuana has no medical benefits worthy of an exception (outside the confines of a Government-approved research project). US v. OCBC, 532 U.S. S.Ct. 483, 491 (2001).

A later, historic *Raich v. Ashcroft* ruling held that the Interstate Commerce clause cannot ban noncommercial cannabis in a state where it is legal. However, a divided US Supreme Court reversed *Raich* on June 6, 2005 in a blow to patients and States Rights.

The Supremes did not address substantive due process or medical necessity, but urged Congress to reform federal laws.

"The question before us, however, is not whether it is wise to enforce the statute in these circumstances; rather, it is whether Congress' power to regulate interstate markets for medicinal substances encompasses ... drugs produced and consumed locally. ... The authority to grant permission whenever the doctor determines that a patient is afflicted with 'any other illness for which marijuana provides relief,' Cal. H&S §11362.5 is broad enough to allow even the most scrupulous doctor to conclude that some recreational uses would be therapeutic. ... [T]he [CSA] statute authorizes procedures for the reclassification of Schedule I Drugs. Perhaps even more important than these legal avenues is the democratic process, in which the voices of voters allied with these respondents may one day be heard in the halls of Congress. Under the present state of the law, however, the judgment of the Court of Appeals must be vacated.

— *Gonzales v. Raich,* 125 U.S. S.Ct. 2195 (2005)

NB: Jurors can acquit without penalty. It is reasonable for anyone to doubt government "facts" about cannabis and its use. American jurors, who reject any case put forth by a prosecutor, and vote to acquit, *are not subject to any punishment for doing so.*

Chapter Seven: Questions & Answers

Why even organize?

You must organize your collective or cooperative or delivery service with a structure that ensures the product is accurately tracked. You need documentation that all marijuana is being grown by the non-profit's members and is being distributed to members only and only for a cost that reflects and overhead and product.

They took my ganja when I got my DUI; can I get it back?

It is a violation of due process for law enforcement to refuse to return medical marijuana to a patient.

What are indicia of illegal sales?

- Weapons on or near your person, home or car
- Illicit drugs of any nature
- Evidence of distribution beyond the cooperative

- Evidence of distribution outside of California

What is the story about bubble hash vs. honey oil?

Bubble hash (water processed) is treated the same as marijuana, as is honey oil for purposes of consumption. But with respect to manufacturing, honey oil is treated the same as meth and can charged as a serious crime.

Q: How does the Compassionate Use Act work?

The Compassionate Use Act (CUA) does not give immunity from criminal sanction; instead, it provides an *affirmative defense*. This can be used as a defense or to set aside an indictment for lack of reasonable cause. The medical marijuana defense negates an element of the crime, which is that the possession or cultivation of the marijuana is "unlawful."

Q: How about searches?

Because the CUA provides an affirmative defense, rather than immunity, it does not allow for suppression of evidence or grounds for reversal if, for instance, police fail to conduct an investigation of defendant's status as a qualified patient prior to conducting a search. In other words, cops do not need to stop a search of the premises for pot even if someone produces documents that prove they are a qualified patient.

Q: How about arrests?

Senate Bill 420 prohibits the arrest and prosecution of qualified patients and their designated primary caregivers; specifically, it proscribes the arrest of any person in possession of a valid identification card for the possession, transportation, delivery or cultivation of up to eight ounces of dried marijuana and/or six mature (or twelve immature) plants, unless in violation of other marijuana laws, such as distribution for non-medical use.

In this regard, however, California law forbids law enforcement officers from refusing to accept identification cards issued by the CA Department of Public Health unless there is reasonable cause to believe that the card is being used fraudulently.

Q: How can I get my stuff back?

You can file a motion or commence a civil action for the return of your seized marijuana or for monetary damages if the marijuana has been destroyed. Penal Code § 1536 imposes duties upon the police to retain the property and to return the property if it is being withheld unjustly. Alternatively, you may commence a civil action for the return of his property by filing a petition for writ of mandate under Cal. Code of Civil Procedure § 1085. If the marijuana has spoiled, the court may require the police to pay damages.

Q: I got off? Now what?

A former defendant may file a motion for determination of factual innocence under Penal Code § 851.8(c). The standard of proof is the same as in a § 995 hearing or at trial; to wit, "no reasonable cause exists to believe that the arrestee committed the offense for which the arrest was made." Proof of affirmative defense may form a basis for finding of factual innocence.

Chapter Eight: Cannabis Commerce

There are several medical cannabis and non-medical marijuana business models, with different civil and criminal exposures, profit opportunities, and margins.

["Medical cannabis" = legal under state law. "Non-medical"= illegal under state and federal law.]

First business model: large scale outdoor grows. This is a non-medical business model with families in the Emerald Triangle who have been refining it for generations and whose grandparents' distilleries in the redwoods first garnered attention from the revenuers.

Northern California middle size and large size growers can get unstrung when talking about legalization due to their perception of medical cannabis being a large factor in their shrinking profit margins.

Current and impending legalization has already encouraged so many new grows, especially indoor grows that Northern California historic supply/demand curve is out of whack. Northern California big dog growers (big dog=anywhere from 125 lbs or more a year, at least in Humboldt County) have seen prices drop from $2600/lb to $2100/lb or even less in the last two years.

Result? Many of them are making it even harder on themselves, competing year after year to grow more than their neighbors, adding further pressure to the curve. It has reached the point that, for the first time, most outdoor Northern California growers are using interstate distribution channels to keep their lb point price from going under $2500.

The U.S Postal service and UPS and other commercial carriers are shipping massive amounts of marijuana every day.

A former client and now a good friend told me, "Odor is not the issue; we solved that; now the problem is shipments not getting delivered because the employees at the shippers are getting better at knowing what to look for, and they just take the stuff."

Another former client, this one in Trinity County

who has been supporting a quality life style for his wife and his two sons and a daughter for almost 20 years growing between 80 and 180 lbs a year, said, "Two years ago, if a buyer even mentioned some out of state destination, I told him to leave. That subject was way out of bounds. Now I am doing what everyone else is doing, moving it east, or moving it elsewhere to where it goes east."

He said he had recently lost 18 lbs to a courier who had been stopped in Iowa for a traffic violation where dogs had been called in (driving in the middle of night with California plates, speeding in a small town).

Second business model: 99-plant grows in certain N. CA counties with permits and contracts in place.

Grows with fewer than 100 plants, under contract with dispensaries, delivery services and other cooperatives is best represented by a retired UCLA professor with an Ivy League PhD who has made it his mission in life to gain encyclopedia knowledge of how to grow in compliance with all Mendocino County laws, regulations, and ordinances; and sell profitably and legally by contract to Oakland retailers. The gentleman also has developed a botanical and herb business that does well and does good.

Some aspects of this business model are so attractive that several clients are currently forming an investor group to do pretty much the same thing. It is legal and can be profitable.

Numerous profitable opportunities exist despite a May 2011 *San Francisco Chronicle* headline announcing the demise of the medical marijuana industry as we know it due to recent federal actions. That headline was in error of course; nothing has changed; there is always some Federal fear factor to this industry and therein lies much of the profit margin for the under-the-Federal-radar "little guys" including "big dogs."

Third business model: **dispensaries.**

Dispensaries, done right, can be cash cows almost overnight; this is where most outside investors believe they want to invest. Dispensaries do have some risk of being shut down, but you can make quite a bit of money until that happens.

Our firm knows of a dispensary in the Inland Empire that grossed $140,000 in its first 6 weeks.

Fourth business model: **delivery services.**

This is the easiest and fastest way to get into the cannabis and commerce world, albeit less profitable than some of the other business models. "Less profitable" is a very relative phrase, however. There are plenty of reasons to consider opening such a service in California and many other states today.

Fifth business model: **medical cannabis broker and/or marijuana (non-medical) broker.**

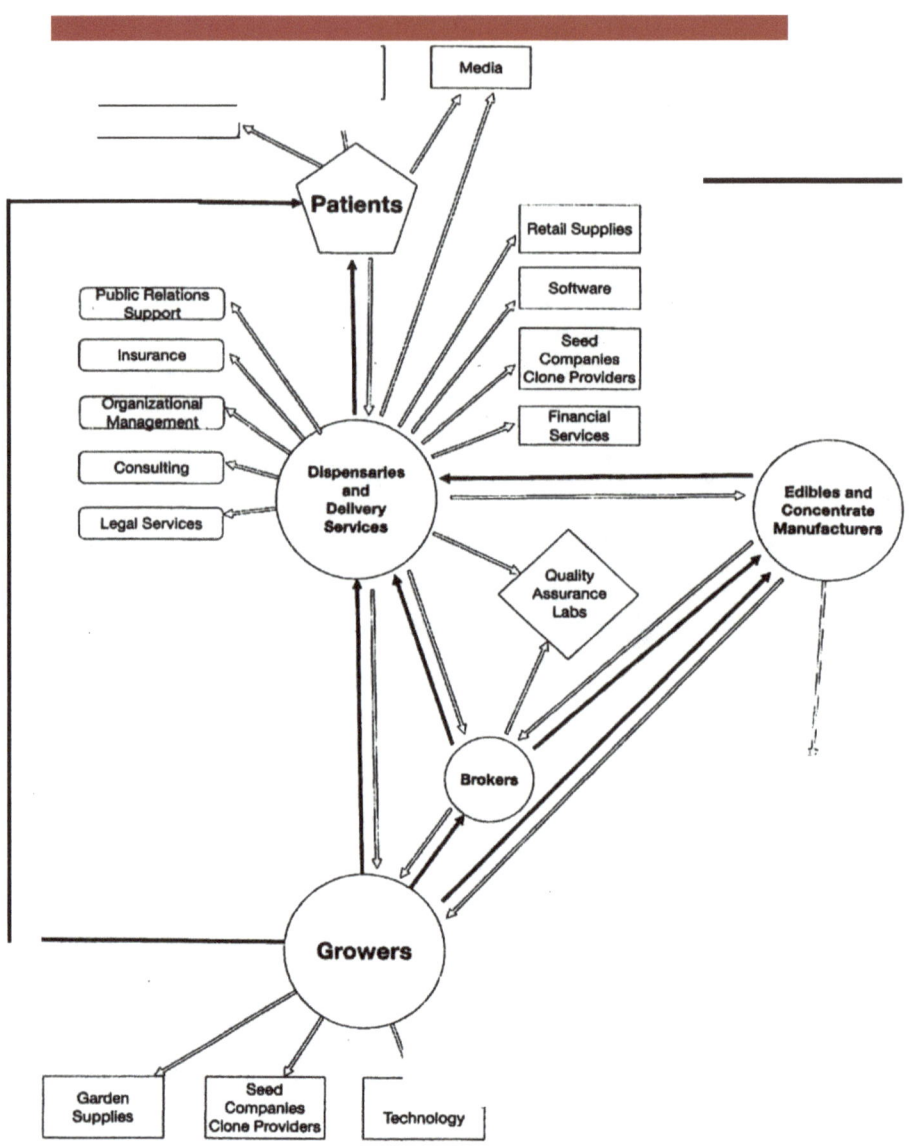

www.ingramcontent.com/pod-product-compliance
Lightning Source LLC
Chambersburg PA
CBHW041111180526
45172CB00001B/208